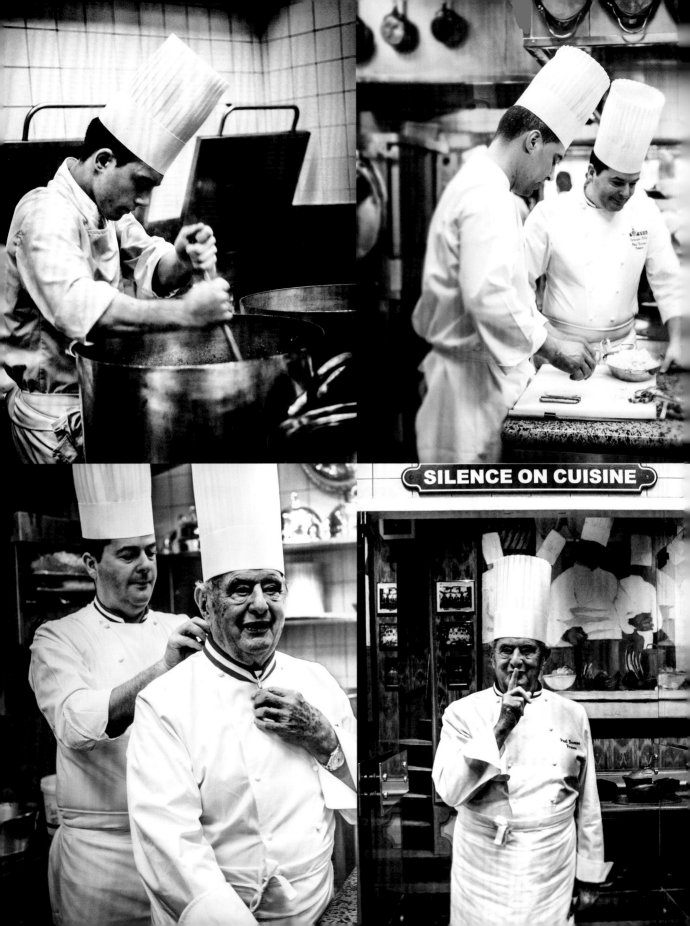

SILENCE ON CUISINE

# PAUL BOCUSE

**Which cooks taught you the most?**

Well, since I was born and brought up in a family of cooks, my future as a chef was already laid out. My father, Georges Bocuse, introduced me to cooking from my earliest days; He also initiated me into fishing and poaching, my childhood years having been particularly difficult.

Never very interested in studying, I was soon apprenticed to the restaurant La Soierie, under Claude Maret, where, since it was wartime, the black market was a way of life.

After a spell in the army, during which I was sent to the front and came home wounded, I was lucky enough to take up my apprenticeship once more under Fernand Point in Vienna. He became my Master and my mentor. It was certainly this man who gave me my passion for cooking and for work well done. After that, working at La Mère Brazier developed my practical sense, and my taste for regional products.

A few years later, Fernand Point wanted me to learn what the big league was all about: He took me in person to Paris to introduce me to the chef at Lucas-Carton. So that was my academic apprenticeship in the great tradition of the master, Escoffier.

**Why did you come back to Collonges?**

My father was getting on in years, and I was going over regularly to help him, but at the time things were not going well, especially in winter, so much so that I accepted a seasonal position at the restaurant La Gerentière in Megève. For the two following years, I shuttled between Collonges and Megève, until 1958, when Collonges was awarded its first Michelin star. The death of my father the following year meant that I had to take over the reins of the family home; a few years later I was awarded the title of Meilleur Ouvrier de France, followed in 1962 by the second Michelin star. It wasn't easy, but with my mother, my wife, and the team we had at that time, we did everything we could to make the Auberge a mecca for lovers of good food from all over the world, obtaining our third star-which has shone ever since-in 1965.

**How do you manage all the establishments under your label?**

They say that where love is concerned, you have to share it. In business, you have to know how to delegate, and I have to say that I've been lucky enough to have surrounded myself with trustworthy people who have understood what I expected of them, and who have known how best to manage the establishments that have been entrusted to them while always watching their development myself, and correcting it whenever it was necessary.

Don't forget that I have traveled the world myself to spread the word, creating places with our French savoir faire in different parts of the globe, especially at Lake Buena Vista, near Orlando in Florida, as a part of Disney World. My friends Roger Vergé and Gaston Lenôtre joined me, almost thirty years ago, to open three restaurants and a bakery / cake shop under the name Les Chefs de France, in the French pavilion at the EPCOT center. These establishments

KEY DATES

**4**

| *June 18, 1945* | *1961* | *1965* |
|---|---|---|
| Marched in the Liberation of Paris parade at the side of General de Gaulle, after having voluntarily signed up in the 1ˢᵗ DFL (First Free French Division) of BM 24 (24ᵗʰ March Battalion). | Awarded the title of Meilleur Ouvrier de France. | Third star from the Michelin Guide, which he still holds. |

are now run by my son, Jérôme Bocuse, who is their president and general director.

**How would you define your style of cooking?**
A simple, genuine approach that relies heavily on the products native from my region.

**How does your cooking develop?**
Let's say that it always remains faithful to itself. Not being a young man any longer, I gladly give my chefs, all of whom are Meilleurs Ouvriers de France, a free hand in expressing this style, which has always worked for me. This is what allows me to keep it on track, so that my cooking always retains its identity.

**What is your cooking philosophy?**
A hundred times in this profession: Start again from scratch.

# GOURMET PORTRAIT

**1/WHAT ARE THE INGREDIENT AND THE TOOL YOU CAN'T COOK WITHOUT?**
Butter and a cast-iron pan.

**2/WHAT IS YOUR FAVORITE DRINK?**
A Picon-curaçao, Fernand Point's favorite aperitif.

**3/WHAT IS YOUR ESSENTIAL COOK BOOK?**
Auguste Escoffier's work *Le Guide Culinaire*.

**4/WHAT IS YOUR SECRET WEAKNESS?**
All desserts.

**5/IF YOU HADN'T BEEN A COOK, WHAT WOULD YOU HAVE LIKED TO BE?**
A gamekeeper or maybe a hunter.

**6/WHAT DO YOU COLLECT?**
Mechanical organs.

**7/WHAT IS YOUR MOTTO?**
"To hope, it's often necessary to attempt; and through perseverance, to succeed." –Gilbert Cesbron

*1979*
|
*Opened several japanese establishments in the name of Paul Bocuse, as well as fifteen outlets in shops belonging to the Daimaru-Matsuzakaya Group.*

*1982*
|
*Opened the restaurant Les Chefs de France, at Disney World, in Florida, with Jérôme Bocuse as CEO.*

# TABLE OF CONTENTS

# TABLE OF CON TENTS

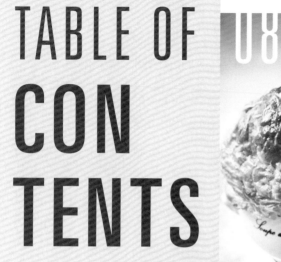

## DUCK AND FOIE GRAS **TART** WITH **ROANNE SAUCE**

40

## TRADITIONAL **BLANQUETTE** OF VEAL

50

## FILLETS OF SOLE WITH NOODLES

58

## **SEA BASS** IN PASTRY WITH **SAUCE CHORON**

66

## RED MULLET WITH POTATO SCALES

76

## APPLE **TART**

84

# SOUP WITH **TRUFFLES**

This dish was created by Paul Bocuse, in 1975, for a lunch party given at the Élysée Palace by then-president of the Republic of France, Valéry Giscard d'Estaing, and his wife. Several chefs with Michelin stars were there with Mr. Bocuse, who received the Légion d'Honneur that day.

# RECICE

## SERVES 4 - Preparation time: 30 minutes - Cooking time: 30 minutes

DRINK PAIRING

*A Bollinger R. D. 1990 champagne, a Frédéric Émile Reisling vintage 2001 from the Trimbach domain, or a sherry.*

- 2 cups (500 ml) chicken stock
- 5½ ounces (150 g) skinless chicken breast
- Table salt
- 3½ ounces (100 g) celeriac
- 1 carrot
- Heads of 8 button mushrooms, 1¼-inches (3-cm) in diameter
- 3 ounces (80 g) fresh truffles
- ¼ cup (60 ml) white Noilly Prat
- 2 ounces (60 g) cooked foie gras
- 9 ounces (250 g) store-bought flaky pastry
- 1 egg yolk

Preheat the oven to 400°F (200°C). Bring the stock to a boil in a saucepan. Lightly salt the chicken breast and place it in the stock. Leave it to simmer gently for 6 minutes, then drain it. Put the stock for the soup aside.

**01**

Peel the celeriac and the carrot. Cut the celeriac en matignon*: first into ½-inch (12-mm) slices, then into dice. In the same way, cut the carrot en matignon*: first cut it in half, then into ½-inch (12-mm) slices, then dice.

**02**

Cut the mushroom heads into thick slices, then into strips, and then dice. Mix them with the celeriac and carrot.

Cut the truffles into very fine slices.

*The quality of the truffles is important in this soup. If possible, choose fresh truffles. Out of season, use preserved truffles. Allow 1 ounce (30 g) of preserved truffles per person, instead of ¾ ounce (20 g) of fresh truffles.*

Pour 1 tablespoon of Noilly Prat into each of four oveproof porcelain bowls that hold 1 to 1¼ cups (250 to 300 ml). Add 1 rounded tablespoon of the vegetables en matignon*, divide among the bowls.

**05**

Cut the chicken breast into ½-inch (12-mm) slices, then dice.
Divide it among the bowls. In the same way, add the slices of truffle. Cover with the stock, stopping at ¾-inch (2-cm) below the brim.

**06**

Roll out the flaky pastry on the work surface. Cut out four circles, 5 to 5½ inches (12 to 14 cm) in diameter. Place a pastry circle over each bowl. Turn the edge down over the brim, pressing lightly to seal it.

Mix the egg yolk with a teaspoon of water and a pinch of salt. Brush it over the pastry. Place in the oven, and cook for 20 minutes. Cut the edge of the pastry with the point of a knife. Serve at once.

*To cut the pastry circles to the right size, measure the diameter of your bowls and add at least 1¼ inches (3 cm). Then place something round of that size (a bowl, a saucer, a metal disk) over the pastry and cut around it.*

**STORY**

# MACARONI
# AND CHEESE

This dish, most often served
in winter, has several regional
variations and is always much
enjoyed by children and adults
alike.

16

# RECEIPE

SERVES 8 TO 10 - Preparation time: 30 minutes - Cooking time: 45 minutes

DRINK PAIRING
*A Saint Aubin, premier cru, La Chatenière 2005, from the Domaine Roux Père et Fils.*

- ❑ 6½ cups (1.5 L) milk
- ❑ Nutmeg
- ❑ Table salt

- ❑ Freshly ground pepper
- ❑ 1 pound 2 ounces (500 g) No. 44 maccheroni
- ❑ ½ cup (120 g) butter

- ❑ ¾ cup (90 g) flour
- ❑ 1 ½ pounds (600 g) thick crème fraîche
- ❑ 5 ½ ounces (150 g) Gruyère cheese

Preheat the oven to 350°F (180°C). Pour the milk into a saucepan. Add 3 level teaspoons of salt. Grate the nutmeg on top. Add ten twists of the peppermill. Bring to a boil over a high heat. Meanwhile, cook the pasta for 9 minutes in boiling salted water.

**01**

When the milk boils, pour in the drained pasta. Let it cook for 2 minutes, then drain it through a strainer placed over a bowl to catch the milk.

**02**

*Watch the milk carefully—it may boil up quickly, without warning. If you place a utensil in it—a skimmer or a ladle, for example—that will keep it from boiling over.*

Rinse out the pan and melt the butter in it. Pour in the flour, in a steady stream. Mix with a whisk.

Pour the warm milk in, all at once. Stir until it boils. Take it off the heat. Taste, and adjust the seasoning.

*Maccheroni is a type of macaroni. Some brands print a number on the wrapping, which refers to the size of the pasta. You can use any type of macaroni or hollow pasta (little shells) for this gourmet dish.*

Stir in the crème fraîche. Add the maccheroni and mix carefully.

**05**

Using a ladle, fill a gratin dish with the maccheroni mixture.

**06**

Grate three-quarters of the Gruyère. Cut the rest into thin slices. Cover the dish with grated cheese.

Finish with the slices of cheese, arranging them evenly. Place in the oven and cook for 30 minutes. Serve very hot, straight from the oven, sprinkled with nutmeg.

*Buy the cheese in a block and grate it yourself. That will allow you to choose good-quality Gruyère with a more or less strong flavor, depending on your own taste.*

# POACHED EGGS
## IN BEAUJOLAIS SAUCE

This very simple dish can be served as an appetizer or a first course. To make it even tastier, you could grate a little truffle over the top.

# RECEIPE

DRINK PAIRING
*A Moulin à Vent Les Trois Roches from the Domaine de Vissoux.*

## POACHED EGGS

- ❏ 2 teaspoons (10 cl) white vinegar
- ❏ 4 very fresh eggs

## BEAUJOLAIS SAUCE

- ❏ 1 egg yolk
- ❏ Pinch of salt
- ❏ 1 teaspoon mustard
- ❏ 5/8 cup (150 ml) peanut oil

- ❏ 3 tablespoons (50 ml) olive oil
- ❏ ⅝ cup (150 ml) Beaujolais
- ❏ Pinch of sugar
- ❏ 1 tablespoon red wine vinegar

## TO SERVE

- ❏ 4 slices from a sandwich loaf
- ❏ 3 tablespoons olive oil
- ❏ 1 sprig flat-leaf parsley
- ❏ Few springs chervil
- ❏ Freshly ground black pepper

## Poach the eggs

Boil water in a saucepan. Add the vinegar. Put some ice cubes into a bowl of cold water. Break each egg into separate bowls. Pour one egg very gently into the boiling water, while turning the bowl. Do the same with the other eggs. Let them cook for 2 ½ to 3 minutes.

**01**

Using a slotted spoon, lift the eggs out of the water and check them by touching them with your fingertip; you should feel a little resistance. When they are done, place them in the ice water.

**02**

*If possible, use an 8-inch (20-cm) pan to cook the eggs.*
*Turn the bowl as soon as the yolk is in the water, so that the egg white stays around the yolk.*

**Make the Beaujolais sauce**

Mix the egg yolk with the salt and mustard. Add the oils, a little at a time, whisking constantly, to make a mayonnaise.

**Prepare the bread**

Cut four circular croutons out of the slices of bread, using a 2-inch (5-cm) cutter. Remove the crusts from the rest of the bread and discard them. Dice the remaining bread. Heat the oil in a frying pan. Cook the croutons and the bread dice for a few seconds on each side, until golden brown.

*As soon as the eggs are plunged into the ice water, cooking stops. It's an extra tip for success!*

**Finish the sauce**

Rinse out the frying pan. Pour in two-thirds of the Beaujolais and add the sugar. Reduce to a syrupy consistency.

**05**

Transfer to a small bowl. Gradually work this reduction into the mayonnaise. Add the red wine vinegar and mix. Add the rest of the wine. Mix again.

**06**

Drain the eggs, then trim* them: Cut off any trailing parts of the white.
Rinse the parsley and chervil, shake them dry, and pull off the leaves. Chop them finely with a knife. Place the croutons in the middle of four deep plates or four egg-plates. Carefully lay an egg on each crouton.

Coat with 1 tablespoon of Beaujolais sauce. Garnish with bread dice and chopped herbs. Surround with a thread of olive oil and finish off with a twist of pepper.

*This little recipe has three strengths: It's classic, it's economical, and it looks good while not being difficult to make. Two essentials: Make sure the eggs are fresh, and watch the cooking time.*

# BRESSE CHICKEN FRICASSÉE WITH MOREL MUSHROOMS

A real classic from the Rhone-Alps region. The poultry from Bresse has particularly well-flavored flesh. The mushroom season is the perfect time to try this dish.

# RECEIPE

**SERVES 4 - Preparation time: 20 minutes - Cooking time: 40 minutes - Resting time: 30 minutes**

DRINK PAIRING

*A Hermitage Le Rouet Blanc 1999 from J.L.Colombo or a 1993 Domaine Bonneau du Martray Corton-Charlemagne.*

- ❐ 1 ounce (30 g) dried morel mushrooms
- ❐ Scant ½ cup (100 ml) Madeira
- ❐ 2 ½ chicken stock cubes

- ❐ Salt
- ❐ 1 Bresse chicken, weighing 4 lb (1.8 kg), cut into 8 pieces
- ❐ 3 ½ ounces (100 g) button mushrooms

- ❐ 6 small shallots
- ❐ 3 sprigs tarragon
- ❐ Scant ½ cup (100 ml) Noilly Prat
- ❐ Generous 2 cups (500 ml) white wine

- ❐ 1 tablespoon softened butter
- ❐ 1 tablespoon flour
- ❐ 1 pound 2 ounces (500 g) thick crème fraîche

34

Place the morel mushrooms in a bowl, cover them with hot water, and leave them to soak for 30 minutes. Drain them and cut them in half. Pour the Madeira into a saucepan and reduce it by half. Add the morel mushrooms and half a chicken stock cube. Cover with water, and leave to cook uncovered for 40 minutes over medium heat.

**01**

Salt the flesh side of the chicken pieces. Cut off the stalks of the button mushrooms. Cut the tops into thin strips.
Peel the shallots and cut them into thin strips. Rinse and dry the tarragon.

**02**

*You must leave the morel mushrooms to soak in water before cooking them so that they rehydrate.*
*It's best to cut them in half to make sure there is no grit left inside.*
*If you can't find small shallots, replace them with two of the large ones called "chicken legs."*

Pour 1 cup (250 ml) of water into a saucepan with the Noilly Prat and the white wine. Add the tarragon, the shallots, the mushrooms, and two stock cubes.
Heat over a high flame.

Put the chicken pieces into the pan and let them cook for 12 minutes, uncovered. At the end of the cooking time, take out the pieces of white meat. Leave the dark meat to cook for another 13 minutes.

*The chicken cut into 8 pieces will have 4 pieces of white meat and 4 pieces of dark meat (the legs and thighs).*
*Make sure that the liquid covers the chicken pieces. If it does not, add a little water.*
*If the white meat is overcooked, it will become dry, that is why you must take it out before the pieces on the bone,*
*which need a few extra minutes.*

Beat the butter to soften* it. Add the flour and mix well to make a beurre manié.

05

Take the pieces of dark meat out of the pan. Take out the tarragon. Reduce the cooking liquid until it is dry*. When it "squeaks," there will just be fat left and the gravy will be completely reduced. Then add the beurre manié.

06

*Soften, cream however you describe it, the butter must be very well beaten to make a homogenous mixture with the flour.*

Add the crème fraîche right away, and cook for 5 minutes, stirring constantly. Put the pieces of chicken back into the pan. Turn them over several times in the sauce, and let them warm up again.

07

Pour the blanquette into a warmed serving dish. Drain the morel mushrooms and add them, together with a little freshly chopped tarragon. Serve at once.

08

# DUCK AND FOIE GRAS TART WITH ROANNE SAUCE

This delicious tart can be served hot or cold. It's particularly good during the hunting season. The one essential is to include either a smaller or a larger quantity of truffles.

# RECIPE

**S**ERVES **8** - Preparation time: 1 hour 15 minutes - Cooking time: 50 minutes -
Resting time: 1 hour

D**RINK** P**AIRING**
  *A Yann Chave 2005 Crozes-Hermitage Rouge.*

### FILLING AND CRUST

- ❏ Skinless fillets and thighs of a duckling or wild duck
- ❏ 3 ½ ounces (100 g) chicken breast
- ❏ 3 ½ ounces (100 g) fatty bacon
- ❏ 3 ½ ounces (100 g) neck of pork
- ❏ 3 chicken livers
- ❏ 2 slices from a sandwich loaf
- ❏ ¼ cup (60 ml) heavy cream
- ❏ 1 tablespoon Cognac
- ❏ 1 whole egg
- ❏ 2 egg yolks
- ❏ 2 teaspoons unsalted shelled pistachios
- ❏ Table salt
- ❏ Freshly ground black pepper
- ❏ 1 teaspoon flour
- ❏ 8 slices cooked foie gras, each weighing a scant 2 ounces (50 g)
- ❏ 2 shallots
- ❏ 2 packages of flaky pastry

### ROANNE SAUCE

- ❏ 3 tablespoons (40 g) butter
- ❏ Carcass and trimmings of the duck, cut into pieces
- ❏ 1 large shallot
- ❏ 2 cloves garlic
- ❏ 1 chicken stock cube
- ❏ 1 quart (1 L) Madiran red wine
- ❏ ¼ cup (30 g) flour
- ❏ 1 ounce (30 g) cooked foie gras
- ❏ 1 teaspoon Cognac

42

## Make the filling

Cut the fillets of duckling (or wild duck) and the chicken breast into strips, then dice. Dice the bacon into small cubes. Chop the neck of pork and the chicken livers into pieces.

**01**

Finely mince the thighs of the duckling (or duck) and the neck of pork. Put them into a mixing bowl with the other meats.

Take the crusts off the slices of bread and discard them. Cut the bread into strips ½-inch (12-mm) wide, then dice. Mix them with the cram and allow the bread to soak up the cream.

**02**

*Order the poultry in advance, explaining to the butcher that you need: 5 ½ ounces (150 g) of chicken fillets, the thighs boned and without skin and the carcass and the trimmings separately.*

Mix the meats with the Cognac, the whole egg, 1 egg yolk, and the pistachios. Add the diced bread. Mix well. Weigh the mixture. Season it with 1 tablespoon (17 g) salt and a pinch of pepper per 2 pounds (1 kg). Mix again.

**03**

Add the flour. Mix well. Dice the foie gras and add that to the filling. Leave the filling to rest in the refrigerator for 1 hour. Peel the shallots and cut them in half. Dice them into small cubes and add them to the filling.

**04**

*The small quantity of flour added to the filling is going to absorb the fat; it does not make the mixture heavy in any way.*

## Making the crust

Preheat the oven to 350°F (180°C). Roll out one package of pastry on parchment. Place a circle 7 inches (18 cm) in diameter in the middle. Fill it with the filling. Smooth it out with the back of a spoon. Gently remove the circle. Mix the remaining egg yolk with 1 teaspoon of water and a pinch of salt. Brush a little of this glaze around the edge of the filling.

05

Lay the second layer of pastry over the filling. Press carefully to make the edges stick together. Trim the pastry to within ½ inch (12 mm) of the filling. Take away the surplus pastry, and put it aside*. Trim the parchment to within ¼ inch (6 mm) of the pastry. Brush the tart with the egg yolk glaze.

06

*Be sure to fill the circle completely—don't leave any gaps. This will make sure the tart holds its shape.*

Press all around the edge of the tart with the back of a pasgtry wheel to adhere the two layers together. Cut some decorations out of the pastry scraps, using cookie cutters.

Make a little hole in the middle of the tart with the point of a peeler by turning it around gently. Mark out furrows on the top of the tart. Stick the pastry decorations on top of them. Make a small ball of pastry and place it on the "chimney." Glaze the top of the tart again. Slide the tart onto a baking tray with its paper. Place it in the oven and bake for 50 minutes.

*The little "chimney" in the middle of the pastry lets the steam escape during baking. The little ball hiding the hole does not stop this from happening and it's more attractive than using aluminium foil or paper parchment. Stick the decorations on the tart quickly. If you take too long, the glaze will dry and they will not stick properly.*

**Make the Roanne sauce**

Melt 2 teaspoons (10 g) of butter in a saucepan. Add the duckling or duck carcass and trimmings. Peel the shallot and cut it into rings. Peel the garlic cloves and cut them into pieces. Add the shallots and garlic to the pan. Mix them and leave them to cook for 5 minutes. Add the stock cube and the wine. Simmer for 20 to 25 minutes.

09

Beat the remaining butter to soften it. Add the flour, little by little, while mixing, to make a beurre manié. Strain the sauce through a fine sieve. Bring it to a boil, then remove the fat with a skimmer.

10

Put half of the beurre manié into a ladle. Add a little sauce and beat it with a whisk. Pour it into the sauce and mix well. Add the rest of the beurre manié in the same way. Leave it to cook for 5 minutes. Check the seasoning.

Dice the foie gras. Strain the sauce again. Add the foie gras and the Cognac. Serve the tart hot with the hot Roanne sauce.

*You dilute the beurre manié in a ladleful of sauce before adding it to the rest of the mixture to make sure that it does not form lumps.*
*This tart is served hot with its sauce. You could also let it cool down to room temperature, then place it in the refrigerator and serve it cold the following day without the sauce but with a well-seasoned salad.*

# TRADITIONAL
# **BLANQUETTE**
# OF VEAL

This is one of the great classics of French cuisine, usually served with rice. There are many variations on the recipe, the only essentials being that the meat must always be tender and the sauce creamy.

# RECIPE

**SERVES 6 - Preparation time: 45 minutes - Cooking time: 1 hour 40 minutes**

DRINK PAIRING

*A 2005 Moulin à Vent Clos de Rochegrés from the Château des Jacques domain.*

- ☐ 3 ¼ ounces (1.5 kg) veal flank
- ☐ 6 sprigs of flat-leaf parsley
- ☐ 1 bay leaf
- ☐ 2 large onions
- ☐ 4 carrots
- ☐ 1 clove
- ☐ 2 chicken stock cubes
- ☐ 1 large leek
- ☐ 2 teaspoons (10 g) butter
- ☐ 2 teaspoons (10 g) flour
- ☐ 1 generous pound crème fraîche
- ☐ 3 sprigs chervil
- ☐ Table salt
- ☐ Freshly ground pepper

Cut the veal into pieces weighing about 2 ounces (50 g) each. Place them in a saucepan. Cover with water and bring to a boil over high heat. Skim* off the scum and impurities that rise to the surface.

01

Tie 3 sprigs of parsley together with the bay leaf. Peel the onions and cut them into eighths. Peel the carrots. Cut them into thirds, then cut each piece in half. Put the bouquet garni, onions, carrots, clove, and stock cubes into the pan. Leave it to simmer for 40 minutes.

02

*It is important that all the pieces of meat are the same size and shape so that they cook evenly. To save time, you can ask the butcher to do this for you.*
*Skimming off the scum allows you to remove any impurities. Don't hesitate to repeat this process several times to get a good, clear cooking liquid.*

Cut off the green and the root of the leek. Split the first leaf lengthwise and remove it. Cut the leek into approximately 1-inch (2.5-cm) pieces, at an angle. Wash the pieces of leek.

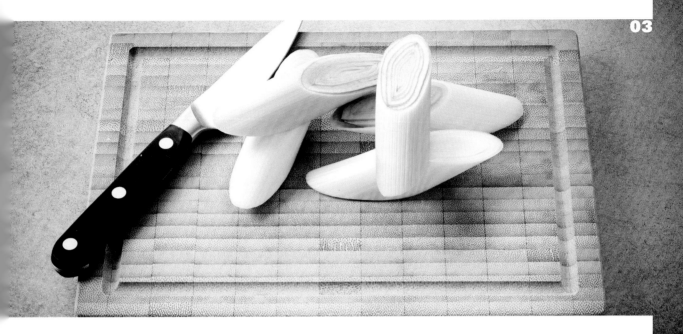

At the end of the cooking time, remove the meat and vegetables from the pan using a slotted spoon. Discard the bouquet garni and the clove. Put the leek into the stock. Let it cook for 17 minutes.

*A blanquette is perfect when you can cut the meat with a spoon without the fibers separating.*

Remove the leek using a slotted spoon. Reduce the stock until there are about two ladles' worth left.

**05**

Beat the butter to soften* it. Add the flour.
Mix it thoroughly to make a beurre manié. Put a little beurre manié into a ladle with some stock and work it into the liquid. Pour it into the stock. Continue with the rest of the beurre manié.

**06**

*Reducing the cooking liquid concentrates the flavor. This procedure is the basis of all sauces.*

Add the crème fraîche to the dish. Let it cook for 2 to 3 minutes while stirring.
Put the meat back into the sauce and let it simmer for 10 minutes.
Pick the leaves off the remaining 3 sprigs of parsley and the chervil.

07

Check the seasoning for salt. Add pepper. Put all the vegetables back into the pan and let simmer for a few minutes. Put the meat and vegetables into a warm serving dish. Cover with sauce. Garnish with parsley and chervil.

08

*Handle the herbs with care: They are fragile!*

# FILLETS OF SOLE
## WITH NOODLES

A classic from Fernand Point, of whom Paul Bocuse was a pupil.

# RECIPE

SERVES 4 - Preparation time: 40 minutes - Cooking time: 25 minutes

DRINK PAIRING
*A Pouilly-Fuissé.*

- ☐ 1 sole, weighing about 1½ pounds (600 g)
- ☐ 1 medium tomato
- ☐ 3 shallots
- ☐ 4 medium button mushrooms
- ☐ ⅞ cup (200 ml) white wine
- ☐ 1 egg yolk
- ☐ 7 tablespoons (100 g) butter, clarified
- ☐ Salt
- ☐ Freshly ground pepper
- ☐ 1 tablespoon whipping cream
- ☐ 2 tagliatelle nests

60

Lift the sole fillets away from the bone. Blanch and skin the tomato and dice it. Peel and chop the shallots. Wash the mushrooms, cut the heads into strips, and reserve the stalks.

**01**

Take the head, the skin, and the bones of the sole and cover with water. Cook this with the white wine, the shallots, and the mushroom stalks for 20 minutes.

**02**

*You can ask your fishmonger to fillet the sole and give you the head, the skin, and the bones for your stock.*

Put the egg yolk in the top of a bain-marie over a low flame. Add one spoonful of water, whisk and work in the clarified butter.
Add salt and pepper and whisk the mixture to obtain a smooth paste.

Strain the fish stock through a conical sieve. Place the fillets of sole, the mushrooms, and the tomato in a dish or casserole, then pour the fish stock over them. Let cook over low heat until the stock boils.

Drain the fillets of sole, reserving the fish stock. Take out the tomato and mushrooms.

**05**

Reduce the stock until there are only a few spoonfuls left. Beat the whipping cream until it is light and fluffy, using a whisk or a mixer. Add the fish stock and the cream to the sauce.

**06**

Cook the pasta for 5 to 6 minutes in boiling salted water. Arrange the noodles, with the tomato and mushrooms on an ovenproof serving dish. Place the fillets of sole on top.

07

Cover with sauce. Place under the broiler for 2 to 3 minutes until it browns slightly.

08

*Watch the color carefully when the fish is under the broiler!*

# SEA BASS
## IN PASTRY
## WITH SAUCE CHORON

A fish with an exquisite, concentrated taste, bass (also known as perch) retains all its flavor in this recipe, thanks to the pastry case. This dish is typical of the "Bocusienne" culinary tradition.

# RECIPE

SᴇʀᴠᴇS 4 - Preparation time: 1 hour - Cooking time: 25 minutes - Resting time: 1 hour

Dʀɪɴᴋ Pᴀɪʀɪɴɢ

*A 2005 white Châteauneuf-du-Pape from the Domaine Saint Préfert.*

## SEA BASS

- ❏ 1 bass weighing around 1 ¾ pounds (800 g), skinned
- ❏ Table salt
- ❏ Freshly ground black pepper
- ❏ Olive oil
- ❏ 2 packages flaky pastry
- ❏ 1 egg yolk

## MOUSSE

- ❏ 3 ½ ounces (100 g) skinless fillet of bass
- ❏ 3 ½ ounces (100 g) scallops, rinsed and dried
- ❏ Table salt
- ❏ Freshly ground black pepper
- ❏ 1 whole egg
- ❏ 1 egg yolk

- ❏ ⅞ cup (200 ml) heavy cream
- ❏ ¼ cup (50 g) softened butter
- ❏ 1 ounce (30 g) shelled pistachios
- ❏ 1 teaspoon tarragon

## SAUCE CHORON

- ❏ 2 teaspoons red wine vinegar

- ❏ 3 shallots
- ❏ ¾ cups (150 g) butter
- ❏ 1 teaspoon tarragon
- ❏ 3 egg yolks
- ❏ 1 teaspoon tomato concentrate
- ❏ Table salt
- ❏ 1 knife point coarsely ground pepper

## Prepare the sea bass

Cut the fish under the gill, as far as the central bone. Split the skin all along the back.

**01**

Slip the blade of the knife under the skin, and peel it back over the whole side, pulling it toward the tail. Do the same thing on the other side.

**02**

*The bass is the same fish as the perch. The first is fished in the Mediterranean, while the second is caught in the North Atlantic.*

Take out the spine by pulling it. Salt and pepper the fish on both sides. Sprinkle it with 1 tablespoon olive oil. Keep it cool in the refrigerator.

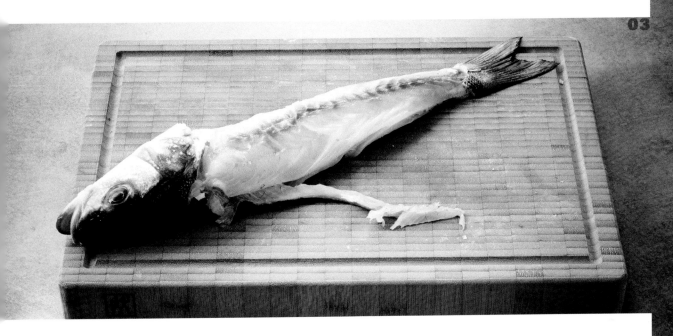

## Make the mousse
Cut the fish into pieces. Put them into the bowl of a food processor, along with the scallops and 2 teaspoons of table salt. Mix. Add ten twists of the peppermill. Add the whole egg and egg yolk, and mix.

*If there is some mousse left over, poach it for a few minutes in simmering water and serve separately.*

Add the cream, mix, then scrape down the sides of the bowl with a spatula. Add the butter. Mix again. Tip the mixture into a bowl. Chop the pistachios and the tarragon and add them. Let harden in a cool place for at least 1 hour.

**05**

### Make the Sauce Choron
Heat the wine vinegar in a saucepan.
Peel the shallots. Make vertical and horizontal cuts in them, then dice.

Put them into the vinegar and let it reduce to dry* over high heat. Reserve.*

**06**           **07**

*You can find shelled pistachios (peeled) in the shops. Cut them with a knife rather than in the food processor, which might reduce them to powder.*
*Tip the shallot purée into a small bowl as soon as the liquid has evaporated.*

Melt the butter. Chop the tarragon.
Put the egg yolks into a saucepan with 2 teaspoons of water. Mix.
Heat over low heat while beating well, so that the mixture thickens (into a sabayon). Take it off the heat.

08

Gradually add the butter while continuing to stir. Add the shallot reduction, the tarragon, then the tomato concentrate. Season with a little salt and pepper.

09

*While the eggs are cooking over low heat, stir them constantly (in a figure eight) with a whisk to keep them from thickening too fast. When you can see the bottom of the pan clearly, that tells you that the sabayon is thick enough.*

Roll out the pastry dough on its paper. Cut two 1¼-inch (3-cm) strips, and stick them onto the sides to form a rectangle (if your pastry is round; otherwise roll out a rectangle on greaseproof paper). Lay the bass on the pastry. Heat the oven to 400°F (200°C).

**10**

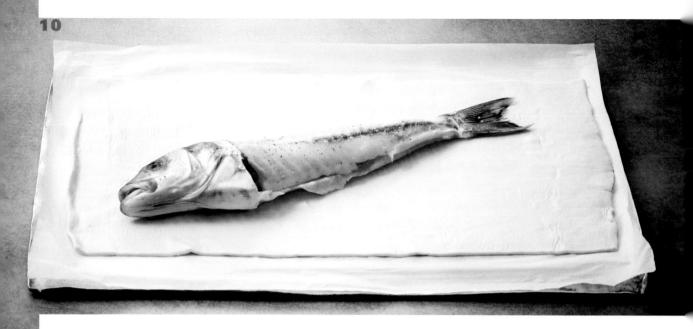

Fill a piping bag, without a nozzle, with the mousse. Pipe a little mousse into the gills of the fish. Repeat this into the inside of the fish. Mix the egg yolk with 1 teaspoon of water and a pinch of salt. Spread a little of this glaze on the pastry around the fish, using a brush.

**11**

*If you don't have a piping bag, use a small spoon to stuff the fish with the mousse.*

Roll out the second packet of flaky pastry. Cut off a strip about 2½ inches (6 cm) wide and set aside for the decoration. Lay the pastry over the fish. Press all around to make the two layers of pastry stick together. Cut the excess pastry back to within about ¾-inch (2-cm) of the fish, drawing in the side fins and the tail. Glaze the fish with the egg wash.

Copy the appearance of fins and tail: Mark the pastry with a ½-inch (12-mm) nozzle for the scales. Draw in the eye and the mouth. Cut a strip of pastry measuring ½ by 6 inch (12 mm by 15 cm). Place it at the base of the head. Cut out a fin and stick it on. Make a small ball of pastry and place it on the eye. Glaze again with egg wash. Trim the greaseproof paper to within ½ inch (12 mm) of the pastry. Slide the fish on to a baking tray and bake for 25 minutes. Serve with the sauce Choron.

*Reheat the sauce Choron by putting it into a bain-marie\* over just simmering water.*

# RED MULLET
## WITH POTATO SCALES

This exceptionally delicate dish requires meticulous assembly, but it can be made by anyone patient. It will amaze your guests!

# RECILE

**Serves 4 - Preparation time: 50 minutes - Cooking time: 10 minutes - Resting time: 15 minutes**

Drink Pairing

*A 2006 white Crozes Hermitage Clos de Grives from the Combier domain.*

**MULLET**

- ❏ 2 red mullet fullets, 14 ounces (350 g), in fillets
- ❏ 1 egg yolk
- ❏ Table salt
- ❏ 2 large Bintje potatoes

- ❏ 2 tablespoons clarified butter
- ❏ 1 teaspoon potato starch
- ❏ Olive oil
- ❏ 2 tablespoon veal stock (optional)

- ❏ 1 sprig chervil

**SAUCE**

- ❏ 2 oranges
- ❏ 3 sprigs fresh rosemary
- ❏ 3/8 cup (100 ml) Noilly Prat

- ❏ 11 ounces (300 g) crème fraîche
- ❏ Salt
- ❏ Freshly ground pepper

78

Remove the bones from the fish using a peeling knife or tweezers.
Cut out two rectangles of greaseproof paper, slightly larger than the fish fillets. Place the fish on them, skin side up.
Mix the egg yolk with a teaspoon of water and a pinch of salt. Spread this glaze over the fillets of fish on the skin side using a brush.

**01**

Peel the potatoes, wash them, and cut them into very thin slices. Shape them into scales using an apple corer.

**02**

## Preparing the caramel

Heat the sugar over high heat in a saucepan. When the sugar has turned a good golden color and is beginning to foam, mix it with a wooden spoon. Add the butter. Mix until the butter is metted.

Pour the caramel into a 8-inch (20-cm) metal baking dish. Split the vanilla pod in two without separating the two halves. Put it into the pan, right in the middle, to form a "V".

*To make a successful caramel, wipe the pan out carefully before starting the process. Move it around during the cooking of the sugar, but do not use any utensils.*
*The caramel should have a good color without becoming at all brown. Allow 3 to 4 minutes or so.*

## Make the tart

Preheat the oven to 325°F (160°C). Peel and core the apples. Cut them in half vertically. Arrange the apples, standing them upright in the pan. Fill in the center, and fill up any gaps.

Place the pan in the bottom of the oven and cook for 1 hour. Check that the apples are cooked. Allow to rest for 10 minutes, then leave in the refrigerator for 1 hour.

Preheat the oven to 400°F (200°C). Place the dough on greaseproof paper, and flour it lightly. Roll it out into a circle about ⅛-inch (3-mm) thick. Lay the lid of the dish upside down on the pastry, and cut the pastry out to the same interior dimensions as the lid. Cut away the excess.

*It is important for the success of the tart that the apples are all the same thickness. Peel them immediately before cooking to make sure they do not oxidize when in contact with the air.*

Prick the surface of the dough all over, using a fork. Trim the greaseproof paper to within ½ inch (12 mm) of the edge of the dough. Slide the dough onto a baking tray, with the help of the paper. Put it in the oven and bake for 10 minutes. Lay the cooked pastry on a cooling rack. Allow it to cool and harden.

08

A few minutes before serving, gently warm a serving plate. Place the pastry disk over the apples. Unstick the apples by holding the pastry with one hand and turning the pan. Turn it out: Lay the plate upside down over the pan, invert, and lift the pan away. The tart is ready to be devoured!

09

*It is always helpful to use greaseproof paper: There is no need to butter the pan and the transfer of the pastry base is easily done.*
*After 10 minutes of cooking, the pastry is still soft. It hardens completely when cool. Handle it with care!*

N en_____ moderne _____ couple ident___ avec panache ____ l'accueil ? Fernand et Mado P___ obtenaient dès 1933 la troisième étoile du Guide Michelin. La Pyramide, à Vienne, l___ gardée pendant plus d'un demi-siècle. Nous devons aussi beaucoup à Escoffier, prénom Auguste, qui, lorsqu'il ne se régalait pas de foie gras en brioche ou n'inventait pas la pêche Melba, codifiait la cuisine française. Et à Alexandre Dumaine qui a rendu fameuse l'étape de Saulieu. On a vu de Gaulle chez les Point, après la libération. La soupe était bonne, mon général ?

# GLOS SARY

## BAIN-MARIE
A dish placed over a pan of simmering or boiling water for the gentle cooking of ingredients.

## BUTTER (SOFTENED)
Butter at room temperature that has been worked to make it smooth and soft.

## COOKING JUICES
The liquid that comes out of a food while it is being cooked.

## EN MATIGNON
Vegetables diced into small cubes.

## REDUCE TO DRY
Allow the liquid of a preparation to evaporate completely.

## RESERVE, SET ASIDE
Put an ingredient or a preparation to one side, to be used later.

## SAUCE CHORON
An emulsion sauce created in the nineteenth century by the famous Norman chef Alexandre Choron.

## SAUTEUSE
a round cooking utensil with fairly high, slightly tapered sides. It is used for sweating foods.

## SKIM
Use a ladle or a skimmer to lift off the deposits that form on the top of soups, stocks, or meat juices.

## TRIM
Use scissors or a small knife to take off the threads trailing from a poached egg. The term can also be used for trimming the fins of a fish or for vegetables.

# BASIC RECIPES

## BEURRE BLANC

- ❐ ⅞ cup (200 g) salted butter
- ❐ 2 shallots
- ❐ 2 tablespoon white wine vinegar
- ❐ Pepper

Soften the butter to room temperature. Peel and chop the shallots. Place them in a saucepan with the vinegar and cook until the liquid has completely evaporated. Add the butter, little by little, stirring constantly, then whisk the mixture to make it foam. Add pepper to taste and serve.

## COURT-BOUILLON

- ❐ 1 leek
- ❐ 2 carrots
- ❐ 1 onion
- ❐ 2 sticks celery
- ❐ 1 bunch parsley
- ❐ 2 sprigs thyme
- ❐ ¼ bay leaf
- ❐ 1 clove
- ❐ 2 cups (480 ml) of white wine
- ❐ Salt
- ❐ 5 peppercorns

Peel the leek, the carrots, and the onion. Wash the celery and the herbs. Quarter the leek lengthwise and tie it up with the celery stalks and the bay leaf. Stick the clove into the onion. Put the bouquet garni, carrots, onion, white wine, 2 heaping cups (500 ml) water, salt to taste, and the peppercorns into a saucepan. Bring the mixture to a boil and cook for 20 minutes. Allow it to cool, then store in the refrigerator.

## GUIMAUVE (MARSHMALLOW)

- ❐ 12 gelatine leaves
- ❐ 8 ounces (90 g) glucose, divided
- ❐ 10 ounces (300 g) superfine sugar
- ❐ 10 ounces (300 g) raspberries
- ❐ 5 ounces (135 g) glucose
- ❐ Potato starch

Soak the gelatine in cold water for 20 minutes, then dry it and put it into the microwave for a few minutes to melt it.
Heat 2 teaspoons water with 3 ounces glucose, sugar, and raspberries to 235°F (112°C).
Pour 5 ounces glucose into the bowl of a food processor, add the mixture at 235°F (112°C), then the gelatine, and mix with the beater. Cover a baking tray with parchment paper, oil the edges, pour over the mixture, and allow to harden for a day. Lift the marshmallow off the paper, powder it with potato starch, cut it up, and serve it.

# PÂTE À CRÈPES (PANCAKE MIX)

- ☐ ¼ cup (50 g) butter
- ☐ 9 ounces (250 g) flour
- ☐ 1 tablespoon superfine sugar
- ☐ Pinch of salt
- ☐ 3 eggs
- ☐ 2 heaping cups (500 ml) milk
- ☐ Oil

Melt the butter. Pour the flour, sugar, salt, and eggs into a bowl, add the milk, and mix carefully with a whisk, then add the butter. Leave the mixture to rest for 1 hour. Heat a frying pan with a little oil, pour in a ladleful of the pancake mixture, cook until golden brown, then turn. Cook for a few moments longer, then repeat with the remainder of the pancake mix.

# SAUCE RAVIGOTE

- ☐ 2 sprigs parsley
- ☐ 2 sprigs chervil
- ☐ 2 sprigs tarragon
- ☐ 1 medium onion
- ☐ 2 tablespoons capers
- ☐ 1 teaspoon mustard
- ☐ 3 tablespoons oil
- ☐ 2 tablespoons vinegar
- ☐ 1 teaspoon salt
- ☐ Pinch of pepper

Wash the herbs, remove their leaves, and chop them. Peel and chop the onion. Crush the capers. Mix them with the herbs, the onion, and the mustard. Add the oil and vinegar little by little. Season with salt and pepper to taste.

# TAPENADE

- ☐ 2 cloves garlic
- ☐ 9 ounces (250 g) pitted black olives
- ☐ 3 ounces (80 g) anchovy fillets in oil
- ☐ 3 ounces (80 g) capers
- ☐ 2 teaspoon olive oil

Peel the garlic and remove the core. Mix the olives, anchovies, and capers to make a paste. Add the oil in a thin stream until the mixture becomes creamy. Store in the refrigerator.

# ADDRESS BOOK
# PAUL BOCUSE

WWW.BOCUSE.FR

AUBERGE DU PONT DE COLLONGES ***

AUBERGE DE FOND ROSE

## FRANCE

**L'AUBERGE DU PONT DE COLLONGES ***
40, RUE DE LA PLAGE
69660 COLLONGES
AU MONT D'OR
TEL. +33 (0) 4 72 42 90 90

ABBAYE DE COLLONGES

**ABBAYE DE COLLONGES**
RECEPTION ROOMS
QUAI DE LA JONCHERE
69660 COLLONGES
AU MONT D'OR
TEL. +33 (0) 4 72 42 90 90

**AUBERGE
DE FOND ROSE**
25, CHEMIN
DE FOND-ROSE
69300 CALUIRE-ET-CUIRE
TEL. +33 (0) 4 78 29 34 61

**RESIDENCE
DOCK OUEST**
39, RUE DES DOCKS
69009 LYON-VAISE
TEL. +33 (0) 4 78 22 34 34

**VILLA LUMIERE**
25, RUE DU 1ER FILM
69008 LYON

**BRASSERIE-REFECTOIRE
DE L'HÔTEL DIEU**
1 PLACE DE LA
MANUFACTURE
69002 LYON

**LE NORD**
18, RUE NEUVE
69002 LYON
TEL. +33 (0) 4 72 10 69 69

**LE SUD**
11, PLACE ANTONIN-
PONCET
69002 LYON
TEL. +33 (0) 4 72 77 80 00

**L'EST**
14, PLACE JULES FERRY
69006 LYON
TEL. +33 (0) 4 37 24 25 26

**L'OUEST**
1, QUAI DU COMMERCE
69009 LYON
TEL. +33 (0) 4 37 64 64 64

**ARGENSON**
40, ALLÉE PIERRE DE
COUBERTIN
69007 LYON
TEL. +33 (0) 4 72 73 72 73

**L'OUEST EXPRESS
VAISE**
41, RUE DES DOCKS
69009 LYON
TEL. +33 (0) 4 72 17 95 95
FAX + 33 (0) 4 72 17 95 96

**L'OUEST EXPRESS
PART DIEU**
ESPLANADE DU CENTRE
COMMERCIAL DE LA PART
DIEU
69003 LYON
TEL. +33 (0) 4 78 95 01 02

**L'OUEST EXPRESS**
SORTIE AUTOROUTE
VILLEFRANCHE/SAONE

RESTAURANT PAUL BOCUSE, CULINARY INSTITUTE OF AMERICA

## SWITZERLAND

**LE SUD GENEVE**
**MANDARIN ORIENTAL**
**HOTEL DU RHONE**
1, QUAI TURRETTINI
1201 GENEVA
SWITZERLAND
TEL . +41 (0) 22 9 09 00 05

## UNITED STATE OF AMERICA

**CHEFS DE FRANCE**
**WALT DISNEY WORLD**
**EPCOT**
83 AVENUE OF THE STARS
P.O. BOX 22801
LAKE BUENA VISTA,
FLORIDA 32830
TEL. +1 407 827 5032

**RESTAURANT**
**PAUL BOCUSE**
**CULINARY INSITUTE**
**OF AMERICA**
1946 CAMPUS DRIVE
HYDE PARK,
NEW YORK 12538
TEL. +1 845-471-6608

CHEFS DE FRANCE, WALT DISNEY WORLD

# ADDRESS BOOK
## PAUL BOCUSE WWW.BOCUSE.FR

BRASSERIE PAUL BOCUSE, HAKATA

## JAPAN

**MAISON PAUL BOCUSE
DAIKANYAMA**
DAIKANYAMA FORUM B1F
17-16 SARUGAKU-CHO
SHIBUYA-KU, TOKYO
TEL. +81 (3) 5458 6324

**BRASSERIE PAUL
BOCUSE GINZA**
10TH FL., MARRONNIER
GATE,
2-2-14, GINZA, CHUO-KU,
TOKYO
TEL. +81 (3) 5159 0321

**BRASSERIE PAUL
BOCUSE, LE MUSÉE**
3RD FL., THE NATIONAL
ART CENTER
TOKYO, 7-22-2, ROPPONGI,
MINATO-KU, TOKYO,
TEL. +81 (3) 5770 8161

**BRASSERIE
PAUL BOCUSE**
DAIMARU TOKYO
12TH FL., GRANTOKYO
NORTH TOWER,
1-9-1, MARUNOUCHI
CHIYODA-KU, TOKYO
TEL. +81 (3) 5218 2211

BRASSERIE PAUL BOCUSE, LE MUSÉE

**BRASSERIE
PAUL BOCUSE**
NAGOYA
12TH FLOOR,
JR CENTRAL TOWERS,
1-1-4 MEIEKI,
NAKAMURA-KU,
NAGOYA-SHI, AICHI
TEL. +81 (5) 2563 4455

**BRASSERIE
PAUL BOCUSE**
HAKATA
JR HAKATA CITY 9F, 1-1
HAKATAEKI-CHUOGAI,
HAKATA-KU,
FUKUOKA 812-0012, JAPAN
TEL. +81 (0)9.2413.5110

**JARDIN PAUL BOCUSE**
SHIINOKI CULTURAL
COMPLEX
ISHIKAWA PREFECTURE 2F
2-1-1 HIROSAKA
KANAZAWA,
ISHIKAWA, 920-0962, JAPAN
TEL. +81 (0)7.6261.1161

**CAFE & BRASSERIE
PAUL BOCUSE**
SHIINOKI CULTURAL
COMPLEX, ISHIKAWA
PREFECTURE 1F
2-1-1 HIROSAKA
KANAZAWA,
ISHIKAWA, 920-0962, JAPAN
TEL. +81 (0)7.6261.1162

BRASSERIE PAUL BOCUSE, HAKATA

The Institut Paul Bocuse

Pedagogical Restaurant - Saisons

Le Royal

Food & Hospitality Research Center

The School of Cuisine

Photo credits : François Fleury

# INSTITUT PAUL BOCUSE

# École de Management
# Hôtellerie
# Restauration
# & Arts Culinaires

## School of Management

The Institut is preparing its students to meet the standards of the profession in an international perspective through new Undergraduate's and Master's degrees in partnership with the IAE at the University Lyon3.

## Pedagogical Restaurant - Saisons

True to French traditions and know-how, the Saisons restaurant allows students to acquire practical experience in the restaurant profession and understand its demands.

## Hotel-school Le Royal

The first hotel-school in Europe gives students the opportunity to develop and perfect their operational and managerial competencies.

## Food & Hospitality Research Center

A Research Center in partnership with the Research Center for Human Nutrition whose principal aim is to map people's relationship with their eating habits based on three complementary axes: health/well-being, taste/pleasure and economics/management.

## Consultancy & Training

This department initiates tailor-made training and consultancy actions dedicated to professionals and schools of higher education in the field of hotel and restaurant management and cuisine in France and internationally.

## School of Cuisine

Specialized programs adapted to all the expectations of enthusiasts as well as those of companies and special events agencies...

INSTITUT PAUL BOCUSE – CHÂTEAU DU VIVIER – BP 25 – 69131 ECULLY CEDEX – FRANCE
TEL +33 (0)4 72 18 02 20 – FAX +33 (0)4 78 43 33 51 – contact@institutpaulbocuse.com
www.institutpaulbocuse.com

## INDEX OF PRODUCTS

# INDEX
# OF PRODUCTS

*Christophe MULLER, holder of the title*
*Meilleur Ouvrier de France,*
*chef of l'Auberge Paul BOCUSE,*
*created the recipes in this collection.*

**DIRECTOR OF THE COLLECTION**
Alain Ducasse

**HEAD MANAGER**
Aurore Charoy

**EDITOR IN CHIEF**
Alice Gouget

**EDITOR**
Églantine André-Lefébure

**PHOTOGRAPHY**
Valéry Guedes

**TABLE SETTINGS**
Sophie Dupuis-Gaulier

**ART DIRECTOR**
Pierre Tachon

**GRAPHIC DESIGN**
Soins graphiques
With thanks to Sophie Brice

**PHOTO-ENGRAVING**
Nord Compo

**MARKETING AND COMMUNICATIONS MANAGER**
Camille Gonnet
camille.gonnet@alain-ducasse.com

Printed in China
ISBN 978-2-84123-756-2
Legal registration, 4th quarter 2013

© ALAIN DUCASSE Édition 2013
84, avenue Victor Cresson
92130 Issy-les-Moulineaux
www.alain-ducasse.com/fr/les-livres

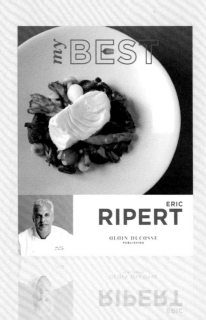